Who Says You Can't Memorize?!

Fun Ways to Learn Bible Verses!

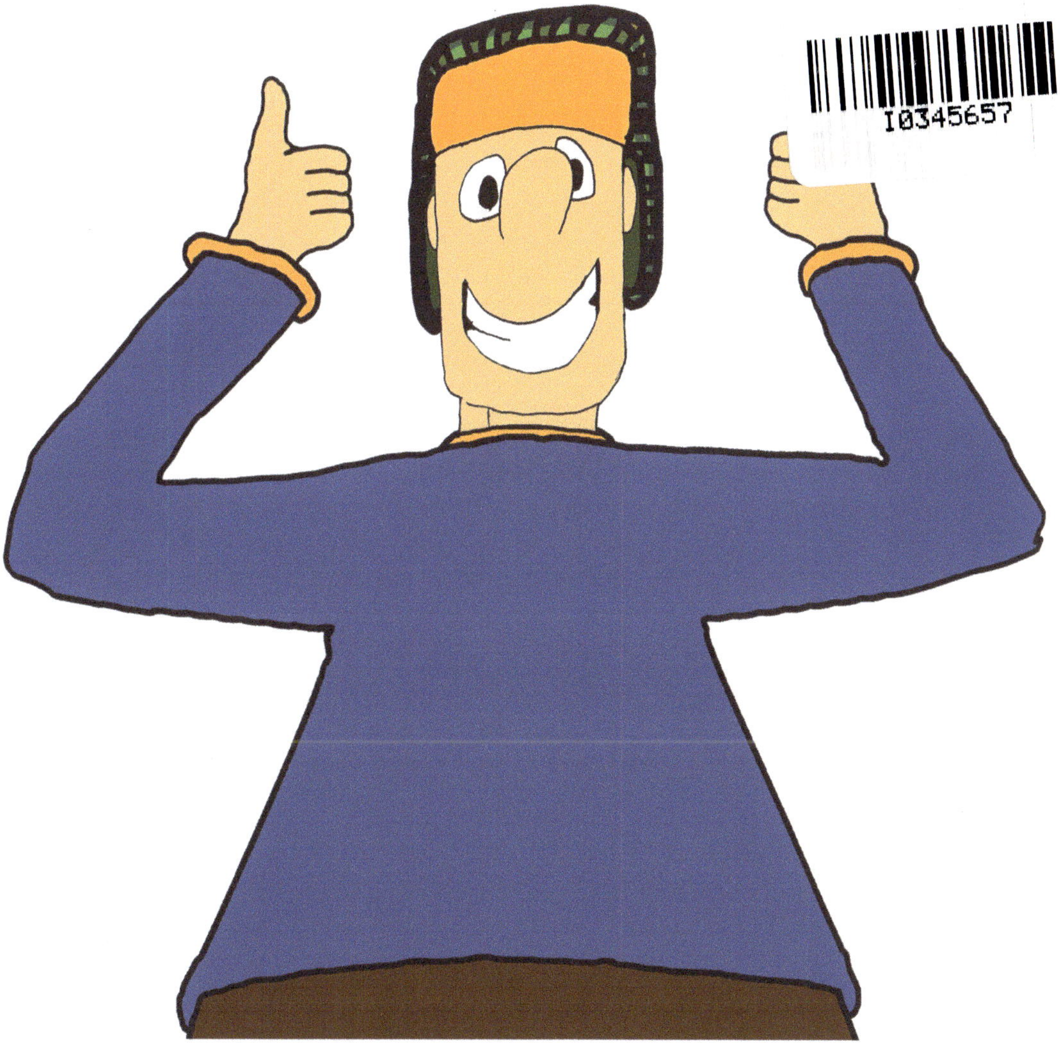

Barbara Bormuth Witt
Illustrations by Noah Robert Witt

Copyright © 2015 by Barbara Bormuth Witt
Illustrations, Cover and Interior Design: Copyright © 2015 Noah Robert Witt

Who Says You Can't Memorize?!
Fun Ways to Learn Bible Verses.

Scripture quotations taken from The Holy Bible,
New International Version® NIV®
Copyright © 1973, 1978, 1984, 2011 by Biblica, Inc.™
All rights reserved worldwide, unless otherwise noted.

All rights reserved. Worldwide. No part of this publication may be reproduced in whole or in part, or transmitted in any form or by any means, electronic or mechanical, including photocopying, recording or by any information storage and retrieval system, without written permission from the author.

All Internet addresses (websites, blogs, etc.) printed in this book are offered as a resource. They are not intended in any way to be or imply endorsement by Lord's Press, nor does Lord's Press vouch for the content of these sites for the life of this book.

We worked very hard to create this book. Please do not make copies of it. If you have this book and have not paid for it, please be sure to visit lordspress.com to buy your own copy. Your integrity is worth far more than the cost of this book.

ISBN-13: 978-0-996-7073-0-5
Printed in the United States of America

First Edition 2015.

Dedication

For my Lord and Savior, Jesus Christ. May this book bring You glory.
- B.B.W.
For God, Jesus, Holy Spirit and Josh.
- N.R.W.

Acknowledgments

This book was a labor of love… love for God, love for God's Word,
and love for God's people who yearn to know His Word by heart.

We would like to thank our epic Father God for giving us His book, the Bible,
for giving us His beloved son, Jesus, and for sending us His Holy Spirit.

We would also like to thank all who contributed to this book including: Josh Witt for his inspiration; Tony Witt for his work, encouragement, support, and insight; Beth Smart, Patricia Lynn Taylor, Pastor Janie Sjogren, Lauren and Rachel MacKay for their edits; Michelle Arnold and Candy Stump, of Claremont Print & Copy, as well as Cathe Graue, Artie Delgado, Jennifer and McKenna Magglio, for their graphics expertise; Pastor Jon and Marites Llera for their godly council and great ideas; all of our Awana buddies; the Mitchell family, the Wachtler family, Karen Huffer, and Alice Hanchar for their encouragement and advice; Maria Kumlander for her photography; our pastor, Dan Carroll, for leading us to seek our destiny in Christ; and Sue Bormuth, for loving us, giving us courage, and for being a wonderful mother and grandmother.

The Lord sent many others to help in countless ways -
please know how much we appreciate you. Thank You!

Contents

Introduction
Page 1

Hey Adults, Read This!
Page 2

Doodle and Draw
Page 3

Get Moving
Page 5

Act it Out
Page 7

Sing a Bible Verse
Page 9

Make Up a Bible Verse Song
Page 11

Crafting Fun!
Page 13

White Board
Page 15

Post It Everywhere
Page 17

Repeat Repeat Repeat
Page 19

Cool Colors
Page 21

More Great Memory Ideas	23
Why Memorize Bible Verses	25
Internet Sites for Bible Verse Songs, Bible Clubs & Memory Tools	27
Tips for Special Needs	29
Your Great Ideas	31

Introduction

Memorizing God's Word is Awesome!

Why? God's Word will transform you! God wants His Word in your heart so He can bless you, protect you, teach you, draw you near, give you wisdom, and help you spread the Good News about Jesus.

You CAN memorize!
You can even have FUN memorizing!

How? This book shows you 10 great ways to memorize while you are doing what you like to do. Combining your favorite activities with memorizing is a great way to learn Bible verses.

Are you active and energetic?
Do you love making crafts?
Is art your thing?
Are you into music?
Do you love writing and reading?
Are you a talker?

There are memory techniques for everyone. Whether you are making a bracelet, singing, acting, kicking a ball, doing a puzzle, texting, making music, writing, or drawing, this book is packed with great ways to learn Bible verses - and they really work!

Pick your favorite memory techniques and let's get started!

Hey Adults, Read This!

Each of us is a unique creation of God, made in His image. The Lord made us to know Him and love Him. Everyone can have a relationship with God and everyone can store God's Word in his or her heart. However, HOW we memorize can be as unique as who we are.

The memorization techniques presented in this book are based on the theories of "multiple learning modalities" and "multiple intelligences." These are fancy words that express the reality that people learn differently. While some people learn best by reading or listening, others learn best by doing, moving, creating, seeing, singing, speaking, or touching. Help your child memorize by using the learning techniques they like best.

Create a Happy Atmosphere

Pray. Everything starts with prayer. Ask the Lord to bless you and your child as you learn about our dear Jesus, Father God, and Holy Spirit.

Embrace that you will do this WITH your child. Be involved with every part of memorizing. Give help when needed. Allow for independence when possible.

Make it joyful! Create an atmosphere of joy and togetherness so that you and your child look forward to being in God's Word. Get cozy and enjoy the learning.

Focus on growing closer to Jesus and to each other. Avoid the pitfall of rushing to complete the verse. Learning each word and its meaning is delightful. Take your time.

Teach, don't test. Try to not put your child on the spot. Don't ask them to recite a verse unless you are sure that they have memorized it. Instead, monitor their progress by helping them less and less as you see them remembering more and more.

Give praise! Praise your child for every attempt and for every sign of progress.

Repeat, repeat, repeat! Frequent repetition is key. Bring your Bible memorization materials with you in the car, keep them by the bed, take them wherever you go. Make memorization a joyful part of your daily routine.

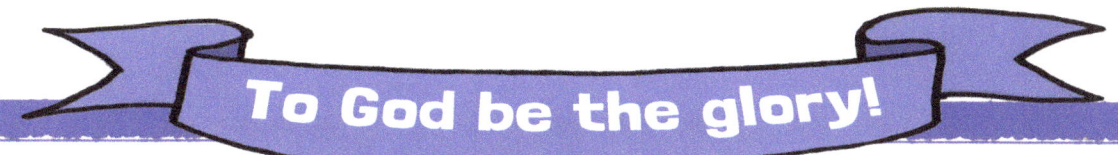

To God be the glory!

Doodle and Draw

God has made you creative! Do you like drawing, painting, or coloring? Do you think in pictures? If so, you will love this memory tip. You don't need to be a great artist - you just need a little imagination. So have fun drawing images of Bible verses and putting them into your heart and head!

You will need
- A Bible verse
- Paper
- Drawing supplies

Pray something like this, "Jesus, You know everything about me, the good, the bad, and You still love me ~ thank You! Help me know You better through drawing pictures that go with the words of this verse. I love You Jesus. Amen."

Focus! Supercharge your imagination and get ready!

Read your verse out loud. Be sure to say the chapter name and verse numbers.

Think about your verse. Close your eyes. Ask the Lord to give you drawings for the words.

Doodle and draw pictures that go with the words of the verse. Write the words near the pictures. Be creative and colorful! Say the words out loud as you write them.

Close your eyes and say the verse out loud. Picture the images and words in your mind. Peek at the pictures until you can recite the whole verse and reference without looking.

Put your illustrated verse where you will see it a lot.

Thank God for His amazing ideas, for making you creative, and for helping you learn His Word. Ask Him to help you understand what your verse means.

You know when I sit and when I rise;

you perceive my thoughts from afar. You discern my going out

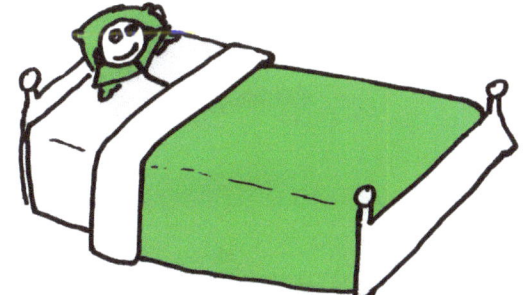

and my lying down; you are familiar with all my ways.

(Psalm - Palm tree - get it!?!?)
Psalm 139:2-3

GET MOVING

Has God given you lots of energy? Are you active and love to bounce around? Memorizing when you are moving is a great way to learn. Why? Moving around brings more oxygen to your brain. More oxygen means more thinking power. When you get moving, you will get memorizing! Try it!

You will need
- A Bible verse
- A place to be silly and active
- Paper and pen
- Stuff to help you be active such as a jump rope, trampoline, swing, swivel chair, chalk or a ball.

Pray saying something like this, "Dear God, thanks for giving me so much energy! Let me soar on wings like eagles, let me run and not grow weary, let me have fun learning Your Word. I love you! Amen."

Focus on memorizing - nothing else.

Write your verse and reference big and bold. Read the verse out loud as you write it.

Decide what to do. Jump, hop, walk, run, bounce a ball, juggle, jump rope, swing, drum, stomp your feet, play hopscotch, spin in a chair, take a hike, dance, or hula hoop.

Get moving and say your verse again and again. Look at your verse when you forget a word. As you move around and say your verse you will remember more and more!

Thank God for your peppy body. Ask Him to shine His light on this verse so you really understand it.

ACT IT OUT

Do you like songs that have hand motions? Are you dramatic? Do you think sign language is cool? Acting out a Bible verse is an awesome way to memorize. Go for it!

You will need
- A Bible verse
- Paper and pen
- A place to be goofy
- Your imagination

Pray to the Lord something like this, "Lord, thank You for loving me and making me fun and imaginative. Please help me to act out this verse with all my soul, heart, mind and strength. Thank You. Amen."

Focus on memorizing! This is going to be great!

Write out your verse and the reference. Read them out loud as you write them.

Figure it out. What movements express the words and ideas of your verse? Make up your own hand motions or try American Sign Language. Use your whole body or just your hands.

Act it out. Practice your motions while saying the verse and refrence until you know them.

Remember the transitions from one motion to the next. This will help you not get stuck.

Practice, practice, practice. Oh, and practice!

Thank God that learning is so much fun and that He gave you such great ideas. Ask God for wisdom to understand His Word.

Sing a Bible Verse

You will need
- A Bible verse
- Paper and pencil
- A device that plays music
- A recording of your Bible verse or the internet to get a recording

Has God put a song in your heart? Do you sing in the shower? Are you always humming your favorite song? If your tunes are important to you, then music just might be the super glue that makes your Bible verses stick.

Pray something like this, "Lord, You created music and You love when I worship You. You made it easy for me to remember the words to songs. I want to worship You and learn this Bible verse while I sing it to You. Thank You Jesus! Amen."

Find a recording of your verse. Ask an adult to be with you while you visit the websites listed on page 27, "Internet Sites." A lot of websites offer great Bible verse songs - just pick the one you like best.

Download the Bible verse song you like onto your device or "book mark" the song's website so you can visit it easily.

Focus - avoid any distraction. When you concentrate you learn better.

Write your verse on paper so you can read it as you sing along.

Sing along and read along with the recording of your verse. Do this again and again. After you have heard it, sung it, and read it a few times you will know it.

Make Up A Bible Verse Song!

You will need
- A Bible verse
- Paper
- Pen or pencil
- Your voice
- A recording device

Do you make up songs in your head? Is it fun for you to create melodies on a keyboard? If so, you are going to have a blast with this memory tip!

Pray something like this, "Lord, please help me to make a song out of this Bible verse so that I can sing and make music to You from my heart. Thank You. Amen."

Focus! Turn off your tunes and turn on your musical creativity.

Make a melody. Ponder your verse. Is it joyful? Is it sad? What type of melody fits? Try singing different melodies with the words.

- OR -

Pick a melody. Could you use a melody from another song? Would a computer-made melody be good? One of these tunes might work: Joy to the World, Yankee Doodle, Mary Had a Little Lamb, Frère Jacques, Jesus Loves Me, Twinkle Twinkle Little Star, or Little Drummer Boy.

Pick a rhythm or beat. Create a unique beat that works with the words and melody of the verse.

Add humor and surprises! Are there any sound effects that go with your verse? When your song is fun, it is easier to remember. Put in sounds that relate to the meaning of the words. It is also good to <u>emphasize</u> and l-e-n-g-t-h-e-n certain words.

Record your musical verse.

Listen to the recording over and over again and sing along. You will probably never forget this verse. Music is the super glue for verses!

Thank God for music and the power of music to help you remember His Word!

Sing and make ♫ music from your heart to the Lord. Ephesians 5:19

TECHNO TIP

Put your finished songs onto your music app and mobile devices to make them easier to access.

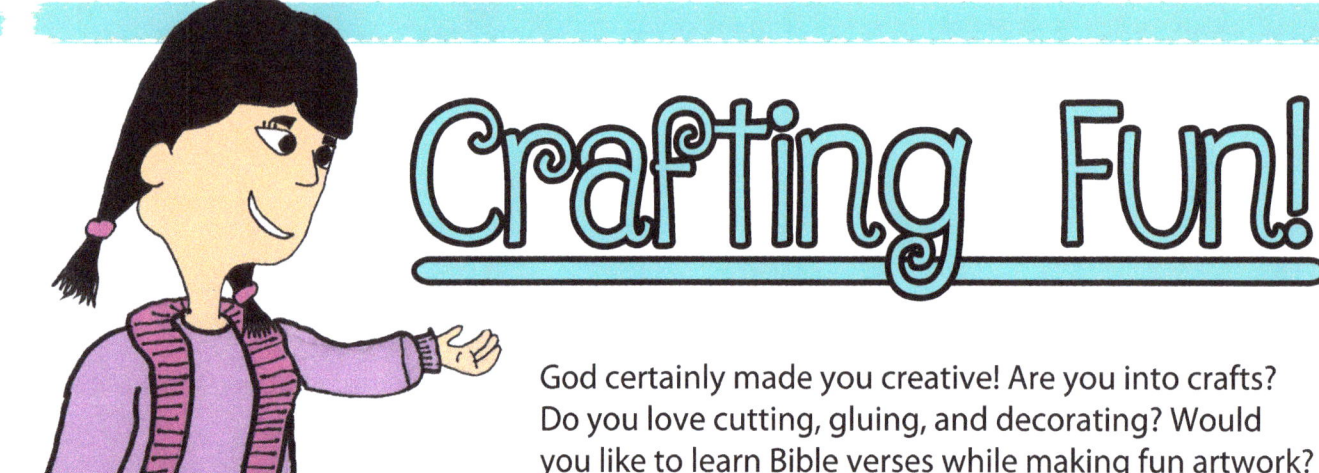
Crafting Fun!

God certainly made you creative! Are you into crafts? Do you love cutting, gluing, and decorating? Would you like to learn Bible verses while making fun artwork? If so, then let's get started!

Pray something like this, "Lord, I love You. Holy Spirit, inspire me with a craft that will help Your Word sink into my heart. Help me understand what this verse means. Thank You, Jesus. Amen."

Focus and read your verse out loud. Don't forget to say the reference.

Ponder the craft that goes with your verse. Ask the Lord to give you ideas for the shapes, colors, and decorations. Think up your own craft idea or use one of these:

Bracelet

You Will Need
- A Bible verse
- A permanent marker
- Craft foam or colored paper
- Ribbon, yarn, or string
- Stickers
- Scissors & a hole punch

1 - Cut the craft foam to fit your verse & wrist.
2 - Punch holes at each end.
3 - Write the verse and reference on the foam.
4 - Say your verse.
5 - Decorate it with stickers.
6 - Tie ribbon through the holes.
7 - Wear the bracelet and say your verse a lot.

#2 Door Decoration

You Will Need
- A Bible verse
- Markers or colored pencils
- Colored paper
- Ribbons & decorations
- Scissors & a hole punch
- Thumbtacks

1 - Cut the paper into the shapes of the verse's main ideas.
2 - Write the verse and reference on the shapes.
3 - Say the verse as you write it.
4 - Decorate the shapes.
5 - Punch holes and tie the shapes together.
6 - Tack it to the door frame.
7 - Say the verse every time you see it.

Thank God for being creative and making you creative. Ask Him for more craft ideas.

#3 Puzzle

You Will Need
- A Bible verse
- Markers
- Card stock or heavy paper (an empty cereal box works)
- Scissors

1 - Boldly write your verse and the reference on card stock.
2 - Cut the card stock into pieces to make a puzzle.
3 - Mix up the puzzle pieces and put them together again while saying the verse.

These commandments that I give you today are to be on your hearts. Tie them as symbols on your hands... te them on the door frames of your ...uteronomy 6:6, 8a, 9a

White Board

Epic Bible Memorizer Dude!

You will need
- Any size white board
- Dry-erase markers
- An eraser or a finger you don't mind getting dirty

Has God made it fun for you to write on a white board? Do you love the squeak of the marker and the fun of erasing? Then this memory tip is for you - it really works.

Pray something like this, "Dear Lord, teach me about Your Word. Make me wise. Help me remember what You have written. Thank You. Amen."

Focus on memorizing your verse - zero in on your white board.

Step 1 - Write your entire verse and reference on the white board.

Step 2 - Say it out loud.

Step 3 - Erase one word.

Step 4 - Draw an underline where you erased the word.

Step 5 - Say the complete verse out loud again. Remember to say the word you erased.

Repeat steps 3, 4, and 5 until every word has been replaced by an underline.

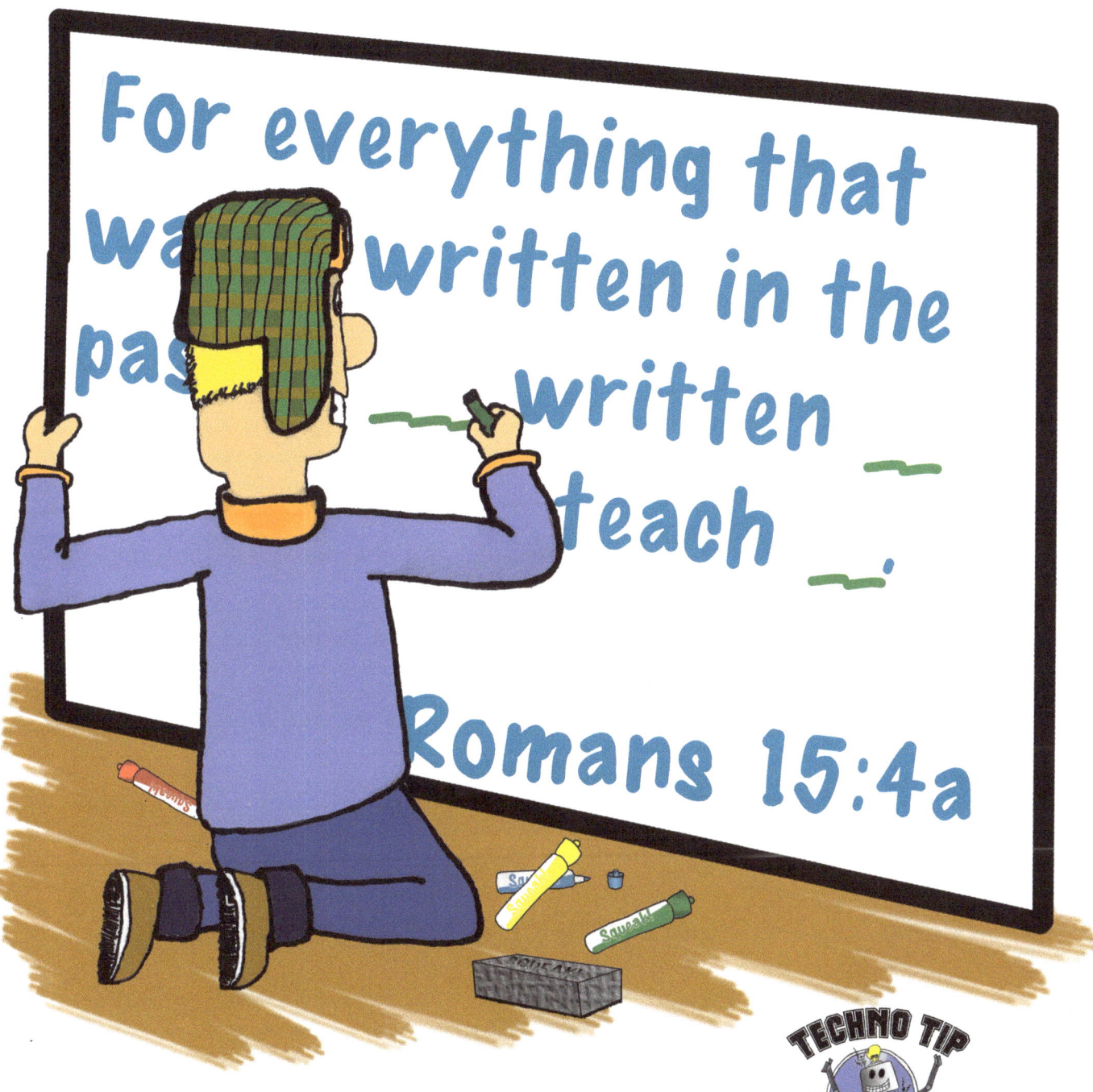

Thank the Lord for the wonderful heart and mind He has given you. Ask Him to give you great understanding of His Word.

TECHNO TIP

Make your password out of the first letter of each word in the verse. Romans 15:4a would be "FetwwitpwwttuR15:4a"

Post it Everywhere

You will need
- A Bible verse
- Post-its™ (any brand of sticky notes will do)
- A pen

Has God given you wonderful handwriting and a love for Post-its™? Do you have pads of colored sticky notes that you are waiting for a chance to use? If so, this is DEFINITELY the memory tip for you.

Pray something like this, "Lord, You wrote the Bible and I want it in my heart. Help me learn this verse and teach me how to be more like Jesus. Thank You. Amen."

Focus! Put your brain in overdrive and get your pens and Post-its™ ready.

Pick three sticky notes that are the same size, color, and shape.

Get a pen you like.

Step 1 – Concentrate and read your verse out loud. Say the reference at the beginning and the end.

Step 2 – From memory, try to write the reference and verse on the first sticky note. Peek at the verse if you need to.

Step 3 – Put your sticky note where you will see it a lot.

Repeat steps 1, 2, and 3 until you have posted 3 sticky notes.

Say your verse out loud every time you see one of the sticky notes.

Thank the Lord for your good memory and for cool sticky notes.

I have hidden your word in my heart that I might not sin against you. Psalm 119:11

TECHNO TIP

Text your verse to all your friends. Just by texting it, it will stick in your head.

Repeat Repeat Repeat

You will need
A Bible verse

Did God give you a love for language? Do you like to read? Do you want to memorize fast? If so, then you have found THE memory technique.

Pray something like this, "Lord, please help me to learn this verse quickly and to understand what it means. Help me to obey You and my parents. Thank You. Amen."

Focus on memorizing! Laser in on your verse.

Step 1 – Say the first chunk of 4 or 5 words again and again until you you know it.

Step 2 – Say the next chunk of words again and again until you know it.

Step 3 – Combine all the words you have learned. Repeat them together until they merge in your brain.

Repeat steps 2 and 3. Add new chunks of words until you can say the whole verse without looking.

Step 4 – Say the chapter name and verse numbers again and again until you know them.

Step 5 – Say the whole verse and reference together. Repeat it all until you know it.

Thank the Lord for your good mind and for helping you memorize.

Cool Colors

You will need
- A Bible verse
- White paper
- Colored markers, pens, or pencils

Did God give you a love for colors - vibrant colors that pop? Do you treasure your colored markers, pens, and pencils? If you like color, this will be your favorite way to memorize.

Pray to the Lord saying something like this, "Dear Lord, thank You for sending us colorful rainbows. Help me to learn Your Word using beautiful colors. I love You, Lord. Amen."

Focus on memorizing and think in awesome colors!

Read your verse out loud. Be sure to say the reference.

Write the first few words in a color that reminds you of the meaning of the words.

Use a different color to write the next few words on the next line.

Pick a new color for every line and for the reference.

Draw a doohickey near the words that remind you of a picture.

Quiz time! Hide your colorful verse and try to say it out loud. Look when you need to. Keep on hiding it, reciting it, and looking until you know it by heart.

Thank God for the colorful world He created. Tell Him how much you love Him. Thank Him for His Word.

I have set my rainbow

in the clouds,

and it will be a sign

of the covenant

between me and the earth.

Genesis 9:13

Take a picture of your colorful verse and use it as your computer's screensaver or your device's lock screen.

More Great Memory Ideas

1
Pray First – God is so powerful - ask Jesus to help you and He will.
Don't skip your prayers!

2
Start Small – Start with short verses.
When short ones feel easy, move on to memorizing longer ones.

3
Be Fresh – Everyone learns best when they are perky, fed, and watered.
So grab a snack, drink some water, do a few jumping jacks, and go for it!

4
Focus – Zero in on your verse! Get away from all distractions.
Quiet your heart and put your brain in overdrive.

5
Build Those Memory Muscles – Your brain is like a muscle -
the more you use it, the stronger it gets.
So, the more you memorize, the better you get at memorizing.
Start by memorizing one verse and soon you will be memorizing whole chapters!

6
Review, Review, Review – Review your verse throughout your day and week.
Review before each meal and before going to sleep.
Pick regular times to review and stick with it.

7
Mix it Up – Combine two or three memory techniques.
Be creative and make up your own ways to memorize. Have fun!

8
Make a Memory Route – Figure out a route in your home and attach parts of your verse to places and things on the way. Walk the route again and again and say the parts of your verse as you encounter them.

9

Link One Sentence to the Next – When memorizing more than one sentence,
link them together by memorizing the first word of the next sentence.
This will help you to not get stuck.

10

Make it Social – Do you love being with your friends?
Make your verse rock-solid by pulling your friends in to memorize with you.
Promise each other to do your best.
Try bringing your verse along with you when you are with friends.
Repeat the verse together and test each other on it.
Talk about what the verse means.

11

Bring in your Family – Memorize with your parents, brothers, and sisters.
Make it a family project and celebrate when you complete your verses.
Try having a memorization race or competition.

12

Joke Around – Be funny (in God-honoring ways) while you are memorizing.
Humor makes things easier to remember.

13

Make Silly Associations – Can't remember the name of a book?
Try thinking of something wacky about the name. Here is an example:
for the Bible book called "Hebrews," think to yourself, "My Dad likes coffee and 'he-brews' it every morning." "Hebrews," "He-brews," get it?

14

Keep the Numbers Fun – Remember chapter and verse numbers by thinking of them
as a time of day or a math problem. Here are examples:
for chapter 2, verse 35 (2:35) read it thinking, "2 plus 3 equals 5" (2+3=5);
for chapter 8, verses 4 and 5 (8:4-5), think "8:45" (8:45 pm) time to get ready for bed!

15

Enjoy Figuring it Out! – While you are figuring out how to remember your verse
you are actually learning it. So enjoy the "figuring it out."

Why Memorize Bible Verses

1

God blesses us for memorizing! James 1:25 explains, *"But whoever looks intently into the perfect law that gives freedom, and continues in it - not forgetting what they have heard, but doing it - they will be blessed in what they do."*

2

God's Word is powerful. Hebrews 4:12 teaches, *"For the Word of God is alive and active. Sharper than any double-edged sword, it penetrates even to dividing soul and spirit, joints and marrow; it judges the thoughts and attitudes of the heart."*

3

God wants us to live on His Word. Matthew 4:4 says, *"Jesus answered, 'It is written: "Man shall not live on bread alone, but on every word that comes from the mouth of God."' "*

4

To know God we need to know His Word. In Psalm 119:97 King David exclaims, *"Oh, how I love your law! I meditate on it all day long."* John 1:1 teaches that *"In the beginning was the Word, and the Word was with God and the Word was God."* To know the Word is to love the Word. To love the Word is to love God.

5

God's Word helps us to not sin. In Psalm 119:11 King David wrote, *"I have hidden your word in my heart that I might not sin against you."* God can bring His Word to you to avoid temptation and to guide you.

6

God's Word helps us spread the Good News. In Isaiah 55:11 God explains that,
*"My word that goes out from my mouth: it will not return to me empty,
but will accomplish what I desire and achieve the purpose for which I sent it."*
Your memorized Bible verses are always available, any time, anywhere,
for you to share with others.

7

God's Word guides us and gives us joy. In Psalm 119:24 King David says,
"Your statutes are my delight; they are my counselors."

8

Memorization leads to meditation, prosperity, and understanding.
Joshua 1:8 promises this: *"Keep this Book of the Law always on your lips; meditate on it
day and night, so that you may be careful to do everything written in it.
Then you will be prosperous and successful."*

9

God's Word protects us. Ephesians 6:17 explains that,
"The sword of the Spirit, which is the word of God,"
is part of our spiritual armor.
If we know the Word, the Lord can bring it to us for our protection.
Jesus himself used the Word of God to combat the enemy.

10

God longs for us to know Him, love Him, talk about Him, and focus on Him.
Deuteronomy 6:6-7 says, *"These commandments that I give you today
are to be on your hearts. Impress them on your children.
Talk about them when you sit at home and when you walk along the road,
when you lie down and when you get up."*

Internet Sites

Bible Verse Songs

"Awana" has Bible verse songs in the NIV (New International Version), KJV (King James Version), NKJV (New King James Version), and ESV (English Standard Version).
Awana.org

"Seeds Family Worship" music uses the NIV (New International Version).
Seedsfamilyworship.com

"The Verses Project" has free downloadables made by many artists. They use the ESV (English Standard Version) of the Bible.
Theversesproject.com

"Walking Bible" provides free downloadables in the NIV (New International Version) or NKJV (New King James Version).
Walkingbible.org

"Hitchcock Family Ministry" has free Bible verse songs in the KJV (King James Version).
Freescripturesongs.org

"GT and the Halo Express" sell CD's of Bible verse songs. Some of their songs have been uploaded to YouTube.
Gthalo.com

"The Rizers" (short for "memorizers") sing Bible verses for kids.
Therizers.com

The "Robbie Seay Band" plays Christian music and has recorded many of the Psalms.
Robbieseayband.com

"Bible Bee" sells Bible verse songs in NASB (New American Standard Bible), KJV (King James Version), ESV (English Standard Version), and NKJV (New King James Version).
Biblebee.org

Subscribe to the "Intoxicated On Life Family and Homeschool Newsletter" to receive the "Ultimate List of Bible Memory Songs." The list is organized by chapter and verse and links to over 1,400 Bible verse songs.
Intoxicatedonlife.com

Bible Clubs

Combining discipleship, fellowship, fun, and Bible memorization is a great way to grow closer to the Lord and to each other. Find a club near you:

Awana
Awana.org

Bible Bee
Biblebee.org

Bible Study Fellowship
Bsfinternational.org

Boys' Brigade (for boys)
Csbministries.org

Hide the word in your heart club
Heartclub.com

National Girls Ministries (for girls)
Ngm.ag.org

Pioneer Clubs
Pioneerclubs.org

Royal Rangers (for boys)
Royalrangers.com

Rural Bible Crusade
Ruralbiblecrusade.org

Truth trackers
Truthtrackers.org

Memory Tools

Memorizing using a website can be helpful. Try these:

"Memverse" - **Memverse.com**
"Scripture Typer Bible Memory System" - **Scripturetyper.com**
"Verse Card Maker" - **Mcscott.org**
"Fighter Verses" - **Fighterverses.com**

Tips for Special Needs

People with special needs have challenges, but EVERYONE HAS STRENGTHS. Your child with special needs CAN memorize. Believe in their abilities!

How to Help Your Child Learn a Bible Verse

1

Pick your child's favorite memory techniques. Review each chapter of this book with your child. Does your child like the chapters with music, movement, drawing, crafts, colors, reading, listening, or singing? See which chapters they like - these will be the chapters you use.

2

Go to your child's favorite chapter. Use that chapter's memory technique to start learning the verse. For example, if your child chose Doodle and Draw, use that chapter's instructions to draw pictures of the words in your Bible verse. Review the verse.

3

Add a second memory technique for the same verse. Pick another chapter that your child liked. Use that chapter's memory technique with the same verse. For example, if your child picked Act it Out, make up body motions. Review your verse using this new memory technique.

4

Combine the different memory techniques together. Use both memory techniques at the same time with your verse. For example, look at your Doodle and Draw pictures of the verse WHILE doing the Act it Out body motions. Review your verse using both of these memory techniques.

5

Continue adding more memory techniques. One by one, continue picking chapters that your child liked and use those chapter's memory techniques. Review your verse by combining all of the memory techniques.

What If My Child Can't...

Every child has abilities and strengths. Freely tailor each memory technique to the abilities, disabilities, and preferences of your child. Help your child by doing what is difficult for them.

If your child can't read, read out loud to them. Use the memory techniques in the chapters with pictures, songs, and movement to capitalize on your child's other strengths and abilities.

If your child can't write, write for them. Just be sure to keep your child's attention focused on the words you are writing. Try typing the verse on your device.

If your child can't talk, use memory techniques that don't emphasize talking. A child can both learn a verse and show they know it, without ever having to speak the verse out loud. Try the chapters that use crafts, writing, drawing, or acting.

If your child can't move, avoid moving. Either pick the chapters that don't involve movement or do the moving for your child. You can do the body motions, writing, drawing, coloring and crafting for them. Just be sure to keep your child's attention focused on the verse.

If your child can't hear, pick the chapters that use their other senses, strengths, abilities, and senses.

Remember...

Pray first. The Lord will help you.

Memorize with your child. Give help when needed and encourage independence.

Be joyful. Enjoy this special time of togetherness in the Lord.

Take your time. Focus on the process, not on the results.

Teach, don't test. Only ask your child to recite things they know.

Praise and encourage. Praise every effort. We all work harder when we feel successful.

Review, review, review. Make memorization a joyful part of your daily routine.

Your Great Ideas
Put Your Ideas On These Pages

About the Author

Barbara Bormuth Witt loves Jesus.
She has the heart of a teacher and has spent years
showing kids how to have fun while memorizing the Bible.
Barbara loves memorizing too.

With her husband Tony, Barbara has two sons, Josh, and Noah.
She has B.A. and D.E.U.G. degrees, and enjoys praying, studying the Bible,
homeschooling, being creative, and hiking in God's beautiful creation.
Her oldest son, Josh, has special needs and they have had tons of fun learning
Scripture by heart. Writing this book was an amazing adventure!

About the Illustrator

Noah Robert Witt is a guy after God's own heart.
He has memorized lots of Bible verses and even full chapters.
Noah is 12 and loves space (the zero gravity type), music, Awana, Boys Brigade,
photography, sports, backpacking, and being homeschooled.
Noah enjoys drawing and graphic design and had a blast doing this book!

www.ingramcontent.com/pod-product-compliance
Lightning Source LLC
Chambersburg PA
CBHW061937290426

44113CB00025B/2938